T0166439

TOUCANS
IN THE
ARCTIC

TOUCANS
IN THE
ARCTIC

poems
SCOTT COFFEL

etruscan press

Etruscan Press
Wilkes University
84 West South Street
Wilkes-Barre, PA 18766

W WILKES UNIVERSITY

www.etruscanpress.org

Publisher's Cataloging-in-Publication
(Provided by Quality Books, Inc.)
Coffel, Scott.
    Toucans in the Arctic : poems / by Scott Coffel. --
1st ed.
    p. cm.
    Poems.
    ISBN-13: 9780979745072
    ISBN-10: 0979745071

    I. Title.

    PS3603.O316T68 2009   811'.6
                      QBI09-600034

Designed by Nicole DePolo
Cover image: *Aerial Sightings* © 2009 by Robert Carioscia, www.solitaartassociates.com

Etruscan Press is committed to sustainability and environmental stewardship.
We elected to print this title through Bookmobile on FSC paper that contains
30% post consumer fiber manufactured using biogas energy and 100% wind power.

Etruscan Press is grateful for the support from the
Stephen & Jeryl Oristaglio Foundation, Wilkes University,
Youngstown State University, NEOMFA, Nin & James Andrews Foundation,
Wean Foundation, Bates-Manzano Fund, and the
Council of Literary Magazines and Presses

The Etruscan Press publication of the present edition
of *Toucans in the Arctic* has been made possible by a grant from the National
Endowment for the Arts.

NATIONAL
ENDOWMENT
FOR THE ARTS
A great nation
deserves great art.

Etruscan Press is a 501(c)(3) nonprofit organization.
Contributions to Etruscan Press are tax deductible
as allowed under applicable law.
For more information, a prospectus, or to order one of our titles,
contact us at etruscanpress@gmail.com.

ACKNOWLEDGEMENTS

The Adirondack Review   "The System of Ptolemy,"
"Medieval Women," "The Cloisters,"
"Good Earth, I Can't Sleep"

The American Scholar   "I've Cultivated a Nostalgia"

Antioch Review   "Oscar Wilde,"
"Mild Worlds Elsewhere"

Barrow Street   "Carnal, Bloody, and Unnatural Acts,"
"Holbein the Younger"

Bridge   "A Troika of Adroit Reactionaries,"
"The Greatest Bastard in Our Literature"

Iowa Review   "Saint Martin and the Beggar"

Margie   "39 Lines on a Theme by Nicanor Parra,"
"Cockeyed Louie"

The Missouri Review   "The Expulsion of the Triumphant Beast,"
"The Sway of One Ocean," "Willie Jones,"
"The Egyptian Theatre," "A Postcard from
Cucamonga," "My Liberation from Vanity,"
"In the Throes of Advanced Study"

Paris Review   "Andrei and Natasha"

The Paumanok Review   "My Desires Align Themselves in Neat Rows"

Ploughshares   "If I Must Be Saved," "Double Indemnity"

Prairie Schooner   "God's Double," "Mountain Jews,"
"In Thinking Range"

Salmagundi   "Maimonides, I Beseech You,"
"Light-Years from My Redemption,"
"The Slipstream of Orpheus,"
"Scaling the Alps," "Milk-Fed, Grass-Finished"

Seneca Review   "The Weather Bureau"

The Southern Review   "The Emerald City,"
"Hordes of Indigent Psychologists,"
"She Loves You"

The Wallace Stevens Journal   "Tonight Wallace Stevens"

TABLE OF CONTENTS

For Cynthia and Ethan

PART I

It is not one person, it is not a few, it is many, it is almost all.

Giordano Bruno,
On the Infinite Universe and Worlds, 1584

My Brother Percy

Embalmed at last after years of snail-paced suicide,
the atheist who checked Eskimo on Food Stamp applications
now rich and strange in formaldehyde,
an acolyte wearing The Serenity Prayer on his sleeve,
buried with his Boy Scout Handbook
and his aspen-yellow Rinehart Edition of Shelley.
Yet traces of the smile he lavished on idle ravioli,
of the cold warrior's rictus he granted to rival ideologies

linger on, even if his quest for the Presidency
—barring resurrection or a Marxist redistribution of capital—
seems beyond the pale. *What is the law? The law is pain.*
Although the State of New Jersey declared renal failure
I've cast my lot with a pair of Haitian nurses who insist
it was death by exposure while pursuing toucans in the Arctic.

LIGHT-YEARS FROM MY REDEMPTION

Catholic in my envy, I crucified every rival—
the satyr, the encyclopedist, the dwarf
Apollo with his rhythm sticks, the diplomat with his pimp's eye
for local talent and Gerard, that non-practicing
atheist with his transuranic lisp and ties to the Vatican.
All for the love of Horst (her nickname since childhood)
who taught me German and other delicacies of Middle Earth
in a railroad flat off Second Avenue,

light-years from my redemption on Mount Rushmore,
the pines tipped with fire as I perused the face of free will
blasted into the granite text of *The Critique of Pure Reason*—
my mind losing opacity, skidding past its music
into deep space where the Big Bang, enfeebled by expansion,
bleated like an act of grace in sheep's clothing.

MAIMONIDES, I BESEECH YOU

A book of Irish hangover cures
        and the *Guide for the Perplexed* tumble in the mind
as the first probes of autumn
        flash through a skylight at the U-Totem Laundromat.

Is it permissible to chase
        the wings of a tiger moth with a glass of goat's milk?

Is it ethical to print entitlement checks on card-stock
        so iridescent that Americans prefer to starve
their children rather than part with objects of rare beauty?

        When I rebuke a student for speaking epideictically
of his girlfriend's ass, is it to say that Satan,
        the angel of rhetoric, is sweet-talking Eve
near the green Maytags, notorious in their own right
        for needing three quarters to dry a two-quarter load?

Maimonides, I beseech you—
        was I wrong to fall in love at the Bratwurst Festival,
to whirl like a Catholic in the grip of a mechanical octopus,
        my face blotched with omegas of rose?

THE SYSTEM OF PTOLEMY

Allergic to the spores of verification, I existed on faith
and Benadryl, believing that your advanced case of promiscuity
had slipped into remission, believing John
when he denied phoning bomb threats to the British Embassy,
his feigned innocence a thing of beauty.

I was vigilant,
never missed a dosage,
never succumbed to the scruple,
never organized my shards of evidence
into a stained glass window of red and violet—

drinking beer on MacDougal Street,
smoking hashish under the Arch until the system of Ptolemy
glowed in the night sky and I stood at the center of existence
loving you and John as I loved myself, without wisdom or recourse.

Tonight Wallace Stevens

Tonight Wallace Stevens seemed deep to me as Crater Lake
and bluer, if possible: who on this planet without a God
defeats death so easily, cuts it down to size,
devours it like an omnivore of oblivion?

Are not the propagations of death bars to pleasure?
If you could wake up tomorrow uncrushed by grief,
wouldn't you feel less foolish? Tonight Wallace Stevens
seemed deep to me as Crater Lake and bluer

than I could stand—for I am drained of blueness,
a boy's face buried in gray fur as winds from the northwest
scour the pneumatic Chryslers of 1959 with sand and snow
and my parents kiss in the street as they did in life—

yet I concur with Stevens that such embodiments of death
impoverish the imagination, that the only paradise
suitable for breathing forfeits its pales and deeps of blue
when ghosts take it upon themselves to burst into passion.

OSCAR WILDE

The proprietor's daughter estimates
the cost of my embarrassing purchases.
The place is paltry and always open
during blizzards or sacred holidays,
where lonely men go
for something tawdry on the Sabbath.

Why, she asks, why
do you carry Oscar Wilde's biography
up and down this snowy street?
Because you're married and can't read at home?
Because Oscar Wilde is so fascinating
and Ocean Avenue is so boring?
Because you love the part where Oscar
pats Walt Whitman on the knee?

As one who blames himself
for the crimes of others, I am too afflicted,
too tongue-tied for the brilliance
she waits for, this girl
roughly the age of Anne Frank,
her hands light upon the keys
of a cash register:
a serious young person coughing sawdust,
standing for hours under a sagging rope
from which her father hangs the pornography.

MILD WORLDS ELSEWHERE

I thought of Santayana, doomed as I was
            to repeat my long history of selling myself short
during an interview with a German publishing house

        for a job I had no intention of accepting.
            Given a youth's revulsion
to old age, how could I, a stripling of twenty-seven, spend

        the last years of my Roman adolescence
            mired in the nomenclature of bodily decrepitude,
seeing the face of Yeats emerge from a water stain

        on the 14th floor of the Flatiron Building,
            the moist eyes of Personnel
reflecting my textbook case of dread as it shuddered through me,

        my legs damp behind the knees,
            my mind split into opposing camps
of self and soul: always two places at once should IRA terrorists

        detonate a pound of Semtex under the immense
            remainder bins at the Strand Bookstore
or should the rebbe Schneerson rise from his grave in Queens

        waving fistfuls of strange wisdom.
            To be somewhere for one's self is hard enough
but to be there for others in the guise of a useful citizen

is to knit
        low-necked sweaters with the femurs of a saint,
to shake the inquisitor's hand while hydrogen fuses into helium

        over the Devil's Tower of 23rd Street and dream
        of mild worlds elsewhere,
far-off rondures of the universe where the fossil fuels of evil

        are depleted, the glassworks
        in ruins, the human-sized jars shattered,
where the flight from God is neither down nor across but up

        into a fake Bavarian village
        with its twin scourges of ultraviolet and trail mix:
verboten to the ones who congregate at sea level,

        where the bookshelves of every household
        are floating wonders of faith and knowledge,
filled with the weightlessness of Swedenborg and Isaac Luria,

        where the rebbe never reaches
        the end of his day as a human being,
resting with one eye open in the dark hours measled with light.

In the Throes of Advanced Study

In 1970 I penetrated the insular world of the Skelquetons,
a tribe whittled down to twenty souls and three acres
of black flies deep in the Adirondacks, where the golden
logos of the inner thigh was reserved for mystics gasping

in the throes of advanced study. Beginners like myself
were tortured, chiefly by means of sensual deprivation,
given nothing of the body but the esoteric growth of hair
south of a woman's knuckle. One week with the Skelquetons

encompassed years of adolescent anguish. Nothing I did
pleased them; they were intemperate judges, brutal horses
of instruction, all my rebellions of thought were crushed
and letters of reprimand mailed home to my widowed mother.

It was humiliating and senseless, much like the year 1970
itself, with its crew-cut Wagnerians in the White House
scrimmaging for power with a German Jew: year of the dead
and paralyzed students, the fog of repellant and war.

THE SLIPSTREAM OF ORPHEUS

Orthodox in my nostalgia for hell
I return to the 1980s via the slipstream of Orpheus,
back to its minimum daily requirements of gruel and sulfur,
to its brown bag seminars on lust
at the base of the Empire State Building,
Fay Wray visible through spyglasses at the top
as boom-boxes blast the Greatest Hits of the Cold War,
including "I Shot the Pontiff" by Ali Agca and the KGBs.

Back to the ash-heaps of thought,
to the statelessness of being Coleridge called *dejection*;
to the fires forcing everything to the surface;
to the workshop for the retarded and Betty Balch,
a middle-aged virgin writhing to free herself from my clutches,
spewing filthy words and reeking of the Infinite.

HOLBEIN THE YOUNGER

Mildred's in the Big House for art forgery
and Claude, our high school Prometheus, is strapped to a rock
in the Peruvian Andes of his locked ward.
As for me, I'm dying
of lost causes on Park Avenue South,
triangulating acts of God for Metropolitan Life,
having come a long way for nothing
since our days of heavy petting beneath Holbein the Younger,

whose portrait of Thomas More
implores me to trash the smut of self-abasement,
to empty the ashtray, to shake
with a passion that shatters the one-way
mirror between us, affording Claude and Mildred
the opportunity to absolve my failures, as I have theirs.

GOD'S DOUBLE

What if God's double is a rhesus monkey
in the emergency room, his mask bunched at the throat?
What if he smells of witch hazel and plays
the doctor-priest to a floor of registered sisters?
What if, with the lives of millions hanging fire,
he uses his otherness as an alibi, refusing
to wear the requisite tattoo?
What if he bares his teeth and points his lewd finger
at the table where you lie unvexed by life?

Should I kill him at close range,
dish out the brains with a spoon?
Will my stomach acids make short work of his sadism?
Will I have satiated one of the three human hungers?
Will the voice of God whine inside the elevator shaft?
Will snow blanket the peninsula?
Will I cease being a Jew?
When his constellation rises over the Rockaways,
will the Bear be Catholic? Will I forgive the monkey?

MY LAST GAME OF I AND THOU

It's the big picture I craved, the peeled rind
of Earth pressed atlas-flat, the weatherman's humid arrow,
the sand-caked globes of the tropics.
I never understood, flew too close to the sun

to desire anything less than alpine breathing
or trysts by the fireplace on the first night of impassable roads,
discarded clothes panned by the cameras,
the landlady dying of old age.

I was a black and gold angel on 42nd Street,
blessing the lewd and the destitute with my mewling poetry.
Look at me now, greasy as graphite, hustling
my last game of I and Thou

in the sunken playground of the yeshiva.
I dribble a stippled basketball, I wait for the blizzard,
I immerse myself in the vat of perfection, I pamper my flesh
with a plush facsimile of Times Square.

CARNAL, BLOODY, AND UNNATURAL ACTS

Mastering plate tectonics was my riposte
when Rosencrantz inquired *how did you spend your twenties?*
The subtext was always drift.
It's hard passing Go in the Andes.
Poor Yorick, booted out of Wharton and now this:
his skull a soccer ball for Shining Path guerrillas.
The lucky get to choose their punishment. I've opted for death
by a thousand tax cuts. As for Ophelia,

Polonius guarantees her sanity. On a lighter note,
when I'm not procrastinating on stage I enjoy a day at the racetrack:
the rotten hunches, the ads for penile enhancement,
the dream of paying off my college loans with enough left over
to cram a mausoleum with digitized artifacts
of a man poisoned by love.

The Expulsion of the Triumphant Beast

Should my *Confessions of an Emu Lover* take flight,
I'll forgive my enemies in the presence of ten Unitarians
then drive west with Vermeer's milkmaid in a paid-for Volvo.
But for now the smoke and fumes of desecration,
far from the lewd subtext of our last date,
when you groaned through every reel of *Killers from Space*
at a coffeehouse within stumbling distance of McSorley's.
You vilified everything I valued,
from the sludge called Odessa Blend to the space-suited
gorilla in hot pursuit of a walking brassiere advertisement.
What dybbuk of weakness hobbled me?
Was it the futurist from NYU with his cigarillo and prehensile tail?
You were the lithe progeny of Ukrainian swans,
your mind and body quickened by stronger forces.

As the house skeleton dimmed the lights,
I dreamt of a sequel based on *The Expulsion of the Triumphant Beast*,
a page-turner from the 1590s by Giordano Bruno.
It was my way of honoring Peter Graves,
a Nordic hero set loose in an underworld of bug-eyed primates.
It was my way of avoiding the skeleton and his tongue,
the rabid dogmatist and his mouth of foam.
It was my way of raising *Killers from Space* into art,
its allegory of alien Hebrews bent on world conquest
vile as the Inquisition that put Bruno to death
for his claims of an infinite universe,
for the heresy of cleansing gods of their vices.
At Chinese noodle shops or over a man-sized burger
at Roy Rogers, I assimilated

Bruno's love for the cosmic femininity of truth.
I cheered his proto-socialism
and sly innuendoes against the Papacy
and though he called Jews the excrement of Egypt
I took no offense, reading it as an understated knock
on a tribe whose anvils of despair sink even the non-observant
to a depth lower than whale shit. We haven't kissed in twenty years
since I walked you home through the snow on Great Jones Street.
I honor your marriage. I curse the accident of birth
that left your first child palsied. I ask in bookstores about your novel
on the shattering of the Cold War into millions
of bi-polar personality disorders. Floating over New York,
I see the Greenmarket at Union Square
where I purchased little sputniks of kohlrabi from your double,

a goddess selling produce in the rain,
her breasts visible through a T-shirt
as ghosts of the proletariat badgered Herbert Hoover,
the Quaker Nero who tossed medicine balls while Wall Street
burned, while its acrobats of capitalism—
who never gave a flying Wallenda about otherness,
who divided their days into six-hour allotments
of grandeur, ennui, annihilation, and lust—
plunged to the earth, their last chance to amaze the gargoyles.
I see Jamaica glinting in the sun
and at the Department of Motor Vehicles on Sutphin Boulevard
I see a pair of jonquils rising out of Bruno's slur
and waiting for Ulysses, their diabetic comrade,
to sail through his vision test.

SCALING THE ALPS

Short of breath and dragging his left rear leg
the rat, a ravaged boulevardier from Far Rockaway,
stands tearless at the capybara exhibit
(his double dead after years of excess), and thinks the zoo
perfect to a fault, a kind of *Theresienstadt*
where honeydews lurk beneath elephantine leaves,
Franz Schubert warbles from the lips of trumpet flowers,
and artificial moonlight cycles on and off

in the moist *shtetl* of the nocturnal house.
The rat drags his oxygen tank into the night world
of frogs and jaguars, that sherbet of noise and heat
too thick for reality, where even the strictest Freudian
succumbs to asphyxia: the Ashkenazi dream
of scaling the Alps, assimilating into thin air.

ANDREI AND NATASHA

In a blow to Marxist thought, our romance red-shifted
from farce to tragedy. I had the paper trail to prove it,
a receipt from the erotic bakery with your phone number
and testimonial to the doctrine
of mutually assured orgasm. The Days of Awe were at hand
and I was grateful for something to atone for.
Years and two lovers apart, we kissed goodbye, nostalgic
for the future as rain speckled our trench-coats.

The Russian winter came early to New York State.
Though corrupted by property and jealous of your freedom
I accepted your collect call, amalgamating
phone sex with *War and Peace*, my life-thwarted prince
dying in your arms as the Anti-Christ reached Oneonta,
the City of the Hills where love began and ended.

COCKEYED LOUIE

In the welfare state of heaven the pamphlets promise
that even cockeyed Louie with his glum Chihuahua,
with the lewd postcard in his pocket
and the Hebrew god on his tongue, with his forty years of drudgery
and his cramped apartment next to the incinerator chute
and his trips to the Food Fair taking hours for a bag
of peppers and light bulbs and toilet paper and dog food,
that even he shall know an end

to the injustice and the carnage
and the boredom: cockeyed Louie, who blessed
the sanctity of unions on summer nights under the vapor-lamps,
cursing the rich while his irritated dog squeaked at mosquitoes:
cockeyed Louie,
who wept for my father at the synagogue, who kept his distance
after Labor Day, whose clothes grew fearfully loose by November,
who by April had disappeared entirely.

MEDIEVAL WOMEN

It's only because I've heard rumors of a woman
who believes that a man willing to drive three thousand miles
to gain even the tiniest measure of self-control
is worth his weight in plutonium
that I stand on this gentrified ridge in Seattle a mere two weeks
after fainting in the Coliseum Bookstore on 57th Street
as I wolfed through a calendar of twelve medieval women
giving birth or prescribing herbs or reciting salacious verse

or haggling with Jews over money, each woman
a mirror-image of you as I lay there in the sawdust
cursing my job at the Institute
where I botched skeins of equations and fueled my lust
in the language of thermo-physics and heat transfer,
superimposing your face over the inlet bell-mouth of a shroud.

The Trip to Hades

It took an Irish astronomer to predict
the dark noon of the soul, that tableau of roosting pigeons
and guilty children mortified by sin.
After the blizzard of Jews abated,
the pope blessed the faithful in Saint Peter's Square,
clearing paths for adoration through the blowing and drifting corpses.
Richie Meade snatched my mother's purse
and seduced my first love—

a long-exiled memory returning to its old haunts
as I grope through the umbra of the cancer ward
with *Ulysses* as my guide,
my mother's diet pared down to ice chips and screw-top port,
her Samsonite suitcase packed for the trip to Hades
under a black sun sweating beads of light.

In Thinking Range

Fires can't keep from extinguishing at this height.
The newspaper of record snags at the tree line.
Despite my first silvering of beard

I remain the child who hooks his God
by accident beneath the Atlantic Beach Bridge,
who fears his line may snap,

who from youth onward relishes the sea
but keeps in thinking range of high country,
a shivering believer, forever letting out slack.

The Greatest Bastard in Our Literature

A flack for the sheep industry, he was the mildest of men—
though at times disconcerted by grainy peep show memories of women
hanged or driven to patricide. It took the emergence
of a usurper obsessed with slashing the social safety net
and desecrating the King's English, coupled with the martyrdom
of Yahoo's Anathema (the slender gelding from France
whose exploits in the breeding shed had astonished millions),
to spur Edmund's reversion to form

after years of running scared with the wrong crowd—
the greatest bastard in our literature sketching bucolic landscapes
during time-management seminars, far
from the contagion of goodness with its rumors of fidelity,
its outbreaks of Cordelias cradled through corpse-strewn streets
by fathers mute with grief.

Midnight Smelting

I swerve like a recovering Communist through New York's Southern Tier,
the dialectical cockfight over but for the memories
and mea culpas, the mind's lone superego
crowing in triumph,
oblivious to the slough of despond along the Susquehanna,
whose shores Coleridge dreamt of in his sleep
when he wasn't dreaming of Xanadu.

He never reached the Southern Tier
nor broke his bondage to incapacity, never mustered his forces
for the grand coherent enterprise:
my hero,
my comrade in dejection, the apotheosis of underachievement,
the deepest failure of his age, the electrifying conversationalist
who bored his friends with talk of pantisocracy on the Susquehanna.

When I hear thunderstorms in the making
over this failed society of equals, I pray for a new life:
my one true job, I've never left it, never been paid, never been passed over.
When the boys cajole me into midnight smelting
I keep my phylacteries in the tackle box and my talk of Coleridge
out of earshot. I lose myself to the heavy water,
to the rhythms of the working class.

On good days I am a walking Talmud of voices excoriating materialism,
taking pains to avoid the skunk cabbages and pink-veined orchids.
On bad days I am at least four decades shabbier
than Eastern Europe, a gray flower of a man who should have withered

away like the state, a true believer who should have jumped ship
while he had the chance, a stargazing insomniac habituated to the Vast,
anonymity exchanged for the higher loneliness of dwarfs and giants.

History jars my confidence in God.
I drive without hope through the Southern Tier (Thucydides
on the dashboard, the Jew of Malta in the glove compartment).
I bear witness to economic forces consummating
their hatred in the sky; I see that rain is unavoidable, that negotiations
have disintegrated into darkness and thunder, that the lights are going on
all over America, scoundrels having tripped the alarm.

Saint Martin and the Beggar

I'm back to El Greco the hard way,
not through correspondence school or a tour of the Prado
or sleeping with Byzantine exchange students
or my dream of breaking bread with everyone from Abelard
to Zoroaster: no,
I'm back the hard way, like Odysseus or Leopold Bloom,
back to El Greco after ten years of wandering
from job to job, from city to city, ten years
of metaphysical dread and meager health insurance,
ten years of death among the fog-chewers and faith-healers.

I hang by a thread to the old cosmology,
loving what I can't believe, believing what I can't abide,
my life in limbo at the tollbooth,
my scarf covering the beggar's genitals
as he cleans my windshield without asking,
the mood of God deteriorating as my Dodge
Colt, unnerved by thunder, races down the interstate past
ball-bearing factories, past top secret airfields,
past miles and miles of denatured landscape,
the saint bewildered at the wheel.

PART II

THE EGYPTIAN THEATRE

Alone and over-caffeinated in this plush tomb
but for a pageant of obtuse, gigantic Dubliners
and the beatific face of Gretta Conroy, paralyzed
by regret as she listens to an Irish tenor (his voice box
raspy as a crow's) and dreams of poor Michael Furey,
who sang for Gretta in the rain then died of consumption.
No getting away from or returning East
to the Temple of Dendur, dredged from the Nile

to sanctify New York, where in love's name
I die a thousand deaths then transmigrate to the D train
humming "The Brooklyn Bridge," a melody teasing
is out of *was* as ghosts throng the airspace of the living.
No getting away from or returning to the sacred
crow of Brooklyn, sacred borough of the dead.

My Liberation from Vanity

Today I preached the gospel of nationalism to hang gliders,
who drove the softest of stakes into my rabid heart.

O fair-haired, broad-minded Californians, how I loved you
for two hours, washing down oysters with domestic wine,

secretly celebrating the end of my moratorium on talking
to strangers holding endowed chairs of beauty or ignorance.

I miss standing halfway down those rotting
steps to the beach, watching you jump from the precipice

before the next corridor of rain struck the amphitheater,
shrouding the endangered bird populations in fog.

I'm the weeping veteran of wars I've waged against myself,
reenacting my liberation from vanity in spasms of

belated sorrow, cocking my good ear to the golden throat
of nature, adorning my story with fifty pages of birdsong.

Mountain Jews

When the lampshade revolved clockwise
its hand-painted snowstorm
buried a family of mountain Jews
and froze their emaciated horses.

And when it revolved counterclockwise
the snow returned to the clouds
and the Jews drove their horses
into the teeth of an ancient disaster

any number of times until the game
grew tiresome or the bulb exploded.

MILK-FED, GRASS-FINISHED

I rise and shine against my better judgment,
my waking moments always out of sync,
always the before and after of ecstasy,
its music emanating from a stringless ukulele
or a Wilson's warbler dead as the League of Nations,
stuffed, numbered, feet bound, eyes plugged with caulking.
I curse the Triple Entente of necessity
aligned against my lust for transcendence,
living as I do in a state of permanent flux—
shuffling erotic playing cards,
relieving motion sickness with mint leaves and marijuana,
waiting for the seltzerman,
a stoic Greek Brooklynite unmoved by history.
Plato would have loved Ebbets Field, on Friday nights
conducting symposiums at the piss-trough,
on Sunday mornings drinking celery tonic,
tossing two thousand years of Christianity to the wind,
tulip-tree blossoms flying over the projects and the synagogues.

This is the sucker punch.
This is the punishment of silence.
This is the sealed pit, the gnosis of shit on a shingle:
the good Rastafarian cradling my head,
the smack of bone against concrete
looping like a MIDI file until the paramedics arrive,
the reefer-clouds lift, and the invisible obelisk materializes.

I have aped the world,

caving in to my worst instincts,

desecrating the Sabbath without distinction or due cause,

rummaging through boxes packed away for the Messiah's return,

my creased footprints at birth

stamping me a veteran of the Long March,

nativity a botched cover-up of my radical past:

strings and woodwinds igniting into Romanticism,

young Mischa Elman selling gramophones inside *World's Work*,

a 1915 periodical unhinged with fever,

searching the no man's ocean of the North Atlantic

for miracles of safe passage.

Mischa, you virtuoso, you capitalist roader,

your black suit three sizes too large,

another Jewish prodigy off the rack, climbing

to the highest station of culture in the year of Channel firings

and mustard gas, the blind leading the blind

leading the blind: I grow clairvoyant

sniffing your dried violets on this day of lamentation,

my juice tumbler serving as a crude astronomical instrument,

the obituary for Richard Nixon five pages long

and still accruing length, his myth gaseous as Jupiter,

the lone planet qualified for self-perpetuating incandescence:

for years I suffered night sweats and visions of Nixon

bursting into flame, his dwarf star

born at the end of history, delunarizing the moon

into an Earth-like homunculus of blood-feuds and anthems.

Sporting two black eyes

and orthodox in my own fashion

without prayer shawls or separating women

from the men, I play the Eroica Symphony over and over
until hearing mutates into smell, the strains of betrayed hope
wafting from my speakers with the sweetness of apricot and plum,
the perfume of infancy.

After a Week in Paradise

Having promised not to apostrophize without a permit
I'll draw no lessons from the red-tailed hawk
circling over this stand of brittle cottonwoods—
other than to say that after a week in paradise

I'm hankering for exile, itching
for the chance to resume my death-haunted ways
in any city girding for attack, as far as possible

from the goose egg distending the snake's mouth,
from the gasping carp in its deoxidized pond,
from the hawk when its hunger spells the swift death
of an animal too common to eulogize.

A Postcard from Cucamonga

Nine slides into the catheter rep's dog-and-pony show
alienation commences, its radon gas penetrating
the mauve and olive histogram of my retirement fund,
an industrial park of assets no safer than safe sex.
As my dying brother said, *a thousand acquaintances*
and not one bastard worth a postcard from Cucamonga.
Dear Scotty: I was shanghaied into non-existence
by a god spouting his Will-to-Power through a blowhole.

From hedging pyrite futures to reading manifestos
dull enough to induce Bell's Palsy in the unvaccinated,
life's a fool's errand, a sequence of erotic pirouettes
ending in abstinence and frenzies of papal hand-kissing.
Tolstoy to Chekhov: *I was an indefatigable fornicator.*
The river mouth is stuffed with foot x-rays.

WILLIE JONES

Watching Willie Jones scamper off with my check
and fake subscription to the only possible choice
from a list of magazines steeped in reactionary swill,
it's soothing to remember that I've been swindled
out of graver things than money, that his spiel

was smooth, lucid, and more ethical than tonight's
Special Address from the White House, and that
Willie Jones excused himself to marvel in silence
as four translucent mouths rose over the rim of a nest
wedged between the porch lamp and the soffit vent.

SPLENDID DRAINAGE

The soldiers took everything: the dog, the viola,
the deed of trust, even Aunt Plurabelle's remedy for impotence,
concocted through God's grace at the apex of the Missile Crisis.
Her faith was simplicity itself:
no minyans or schismatics, no chastening rods
or human sacrifice, only the Divine Word untamed by exegesis,
unamplified by a bullhorn: the voice Plurabelle
heard at the planetarium when the black insect

dipped into its hoard of starry nights,
exposing heaven to scores of peeping agnostics.
After the war I toiled as a payload specialist for NASA,
fooling no one but myself as I crammed infinity into nutshells,
willing, if need be, to shuck it all for martyrdom, prophesying
weightlessness without space suits or bone loss.

A Troika of Adroit Reactionaries

Lacking forethought or a line of credit,
I joined forces with malcontents
at the tree line of globalization: no aquavit,
no sex for the road.

Subsisting on tubes of yogurt,
we shivered in the frozen fog
as the old plied us with lies
timed to erupt as truth in our dreams—

as when a troika of adroit reactionaries
are caught in flagrante delicto
at an orphanage for abandoned instincts

or when a helicopter packed with torturers
slams into a monolith of nesting puffins,
none of whom are seriously injured.

UNEARTHLY JOY

She was shot in the neck and right breast
after surrendering her stacks of tens and twenties
to a teenaged Ostrogoth flunking algebra.

An hour before it happened,
I was too busy scourging myself to acknowledge her smile
after my deposit, to ask why her face,

half-Greek and half-Persian, whose eyes
had seen more than their share of barbarians at the gate,
glowed with unearthly joy

at the drive-in window of a bank branch
at the edge of an industrial park
beneath the four shadows of a cloverleaf.

If only I had dragged her away for a cup of coffee
at Denny's, I could have changed history—
had I been strong enough, had I mustered

the ten tribes of my being, had I cast my finger shadows
on the table as a way of asking why such radiance
was on a Monday morning marked for death.

EXCHANGING BISHOPS

The house reeked of Lucky Strikes as I read your hypothesis
on the death of small talk in waiting rooms.

Though our notion of romance
was a blitz of moves across a magnetized chessboard,
rumors proliferated in ways that only an arms race analyst could love

and the truth, which neither of us had the courage
to keep secret, found no defender.

39 Lines on a Theme by Nicanor Parra

Since man's life is nothing but a bit of action at a distance,
I'm rereading Isaac Newton's life for the seventh time.
It is my specialty, my evasion, all this conjecturing
about his loneliness and crabbed nature, when the real question
lurks in the closet or behind the dumpster glistening with rain.
The real question, if asked in public, charges you
with the magnetism of Orpheus,
the metallic whores of Dionysus
arriving from all directions, tearing you apart for asking
why evil afflicts the innocent and who sanctions it,
blighting the orchards, exposing itself
to children, driving the elderly
mad on park benches?

To this God replied
Since trees are nothing but moving trees,
nothing but chairs and tables in perpetual motion,
since prose is the change to rain after a night of poetry,
I can speak with authority while inhaling fumes
at bus stops or inside padded rooms;
nothing escapes my purview, not even your wife or bank account
or the number of faded roses perfuming your memory.
What is your spiritual dignity to me,
I who watched without emotion the bludgeoning of cities
and young mothers savaged on television.
What is pain to me, a satyr lounging in the nude,
who owes to the shore's wisdom his charred spine of driftwood?

There is no salvation, no third way,
only our visions of death-in-life or life-in-death
seen through smudged windows on the southbound D train,
Mother Russia extracting her pancreas
by candlelight, America holding itself hostage
for three nights inside the Presidential suite at the Waldorf,
ripped on Benzedrine, crunching pornographic
spreadsheets, dialing sex.
Yet *since there is also a heaven in hell,*
I feel like singing, however quietly: a few hours ago
the cello recital ended, the *Kol Nidre* delivering
its afterbirth of silence as they marched us from the auditorium,
our wingless ankles at the mercy of flashlights.

My Desires Align Themselves in Neat Rows

When I see a woman at the Cottage Bakery
immersed in *Ulysses* or *The Brothers Karamazov*
my desires align themselves in neat rows

for the march into liberated Paris—we do not
speak, it would destroy the delicate balance
of our agendas for truth and beauty

(in love the best goes unspoken, reflective
as mulled cider)—her eyes catching mine in the act,
mine feigning interest in yesterday's pastries.

THE EMERALD CITY

I'll thunder Blake's "Jerusalem" until Security drags me feetfirst
from this corporate lavatory, my ten stolen minutes of the imagination
doused forever, having consumed nothing but the smallest
denomination of billable time, for which my punishment
will be too lenient to bear.

Forgive my soul's incontinence, the sky stained
east to west from an experiment gone awry with vials of copper sulfate,
dusk over the opera house
as I push the envelope of decorum with offstage hernia coughs
during a performance of *Tannhäuser*. Dying here

is to suffer from a rare form of health, to watch the Space Needle
emptied of its vaccine, the mind inoculated against pandemics of reality.
To die here is to learn what is learned where others live—
that the end is dark as our friends are false, that even lovely hills
harbor gas pipes belching fire.

ATROCIOUS PHILOSOPHY

Atrocious philosophy at thirty thousand feet,
so many chewed to pieces by the fanged *Weltgeist* of Hegel,
an idea so vile
it could only have germinated
in the dehydrated regions of a mind
suffering for privacy and leg space,
warped by salty crackers and this God's-eye view of space,
its meteor showers and consolations of nothingness.

It is one thing to hate our midnight snack
but quite another to devour the innocent.
We know the face of luck when we see it, its mild features
assuaging our terror as we brace
for a forced landing among strangers, not saved
as we imagined but at least delivered to indifferent hands.

VACATIONS

I

Lurching through Prague on her stilts of war and lechery,
Eugenia joined an ensemble of dwarfs
staging a street pantomime of *Troilus and Cressida*,
the crowd dispersing like seeds in brisk wind.

II

Here come the Japanese speed walkers rippling
the paper lanterns of August 6th, day of the hideous
sun demon—there is a cubicle in North America
whose partitions bear my burnt shadow.

III

I love the ravine-deep introspection of women
lost in the temperate rainforest of their late thirties.

IV

At scenic overlooks dotting the Hayden Valley
marriages totter like new-born ungulates.

V

When the mist shears off Grand Prismatic Spring
all paths lead to the half-devoured child.

The Sway of One Ocean

My thanks to South Dakota Public Radio
for injecting Hector Berlioz into the nothingness
between Sioux Falls and Rapid City.
At the wheel I'm Neo-platonic to the extreme,
a party of one having long since excommunicated the many.

With no thoughts of turning back, I disappear
into this vast eroded prospect, my mental traveling complete,
my marriage to these Badlands now consummated in body,
the sway of one ocean giving way to another,
to the smack of new waters against an unrecognizable shore.

But for the Rumors of Peace

Deliver me from the earthshaking obituaries
of giant plant eaters keeling over from loneliness,
of genocidal monsters dying in their sleep—
no one foolish or vile enough
to distract me from the outrage of youth cut short
or the celebration of purposeful longevity.

There is always one Jew left to untangle
the meaning of his life when Christmas ends,
when the little doors close behind the songbirds,
when cellos are put to bed for the long starless night.

On a local station known for its reprehensible
political bias, Alistair Sim plays Scrooge to a fault,
as if desiring us to take his passage
from greed to benevolence with a pillar of salt.
O fog and pink lamplight, drizzle and melting snow:
but for the rumors of peace I would be the happiest of men.

HORDES OF INDIGENT PSYCHOLOGISTS

Hours after my decision to defect, the elders of the West
blamed me for the drought and the power failure. Monopolists at heart,
it was they who gouged the price of remaining
to prohibitive levels. I've outgrown the sequoia. I've ogled
my last Joan of Arc at the drive-in *auto da fé*.

Time to release my daemon on its own recognizance,
to resuscitate my dream of staging *The Ring* cycle in its original Yiddish
or inciting riots among hordes of indigent psychologists
practicing in squalor under the viaduct.

Bald as my tires, I haven't hugged the road in years.
But why disclose my lusts to gluttons for titillation?
Better to misread a cluster of thunderheads building
east of Des Moines for the tops of the Olympic Mountains, my life
at forty beginning *in medias res* of a price war between rival masseuses.

PART III

Double Indemnity

Transparent as a think-tank fantasia,
my dream of April expands its empire without resentment,
dissolving all estrangements into an intimacy
that makes a god out of difference,
equating Madonna Ciccione's torment on *Biography*

with Blake's engravings of the *Inferno*—
an amalgam of awe and abhorrence at times
beatifying the damned.
Next week the secret life of Jesus,
his trip to Japan where he devoured the Buddha.

The liquid crystals of caller ID spell Sears,
on whose raft of credit I sail the river Styx without fear,
waving my unexpired maintenance agreements.
Expire: that vile euphemism. I've watched it lay waste
entire aisles of dairy products.

I've touched its Braille stippling
on your bare shoulder as we sank into corruption
á la Stanwick and MacMurray in *Double Indemnity*—
their eyes the only hint of light as they lusted
through dark Los Angeles, extracting nothingness

from the oxides of being. Your hair is long
as a winter night in Iowa. I whisper to the damned
that strands of gray are both the metaphor
and the enactment of change, that visions of paradise
thin the atmosphere, coaxing the aurora to slip

southward, its scarves of light
distracting us from the holy orders of flesh—
Blake's whirlwind of lovers in their white-hot plasma,
Madonna's critics smelling blood
in their netherworld of paparazzi and prey.

Your hair is as lustrous as a child's.
You hold the small of your back as if to stave off time—
staving off time. I spent my youth devising ways
to merge parallel lives, cadging graph paper in cafeterias
to plot the coordinates of what might heed or ignore

my prayers for rescue, my right-angled
mind almost Christian in its lust for changing course
with the abrupt finality of a moment's notice—
as when kindred souls, their bodies touching for the first time,
transmute desire into fate.

GOOD EARTH, I CAN'T SLEEP

I unbuckled the Atrocity Belt of the Balkans
but my discomfort grew worse.
I ripped the boot of Italy from my foot
but the infection spread to my calf.

Though I pass the kidney stones of England,
though I endure high colonics to cleanse myself
of France, what I fear most is losing Russia
to a surgeon's saw in the Crimea.

I'd steal codeine from dental cripples
to outflank the phantom pain of the empire
before it reaches the sciatic nerve of India.
Willing to try anything for relief, I sniff glue

and coriander for traces of Heaven
but it doesn't work and always there is China
to tremble over, an affliction of the brain
I'm years from accepting rationally. Good Earth,

I can't sleep. Numb me with love and opium.

FROM THE VISIONS OF WILLIAM BLAKE

In the parking lot of the Food Giant
I kneel beside my sleeping infant, his features
appropriated by nature from the visions of William Blake,
the veined eyelids nearly transparent, palpitating with residual brightness.

The Weather Bureau

Just when I thought Romanticism was finished
and the mind and body gas stations of dyspepsia and dogmatism,
evidence to the contrary filtered through the madroñas.

The moon had devoured most of the sun's light
but I knew from experience that short of a total eclipse
all catastrophes are private, on the order of hives or a sudden

loss of desire. The leaves revealed the sun's
weakness, its crescent shape resolving into hundreds
of crisp images on the ground as I listened to the wind chimes

and watched a woman fall to her hands and knees
to read a passage from *Moby Dick* chipped into the foot-bridge
that connected Magnuson Park

with an enclave housing the Weather Bureau,
whose glass walls mirrored the anemic sky until my first day
as a citizen of the imagination faded to neutrality.

She Loves You

She sleeps upstairs in our son's bedroom,
last pocket of warmth in a pitch-dark house.
Where's the matchbook I saved for this contingency—
the light of the known universe under house arrest
beyond the scrutiny of telescopes, vanished
but with a flash that reveals my invisible world of utensils,
the crystals of my abrasive cleansers.
This blackout stinks of politics.

I am not a member of the Donner Party;
I have cans and can openers. The milk won't sour. I've lodged
the cartons in the snow, tilting them to induce vertigo in squirrels,
to simulate Berlin during the Weimar Republic,
its skyline a histogram of betrayed ideals. No places but in events.
If worse comes to worst, I'll build a ragtag army of light
out of broken Chanukah candles and the blob of wax left over
from my Christmas Eve with the radical Baptists.

I thumb through my wife's opera magazines,
comparing my sorrow to Werther's, the guttering candles
playing cat and mouse with the absurd plot as gales from the East
glaze the kitchen window with ice. I am not Scott
of the Antarctic. Wastelands survive without me, as this night
will survive the dawn—why not, Lenin is Ozymandias: anything can happen.
When I smile or arch my brow the edifice of Catholicism
suffers structural damage,

its emissaries fanning out in all directions,
the Pope found sleepwalking inside the Holocaust Museum,

conducting interfaith dialogues with boxes of hair and shoes.
I need candles and music to civilize my mind,
to touch the newborn states of 1989, when the sutures
at the heart of Europe melted into the wound, when my wife,
nine months pregnant, wept as Werther sang himself to death
on a stage glowing with hundreds of candles.

Werther, blessed with my distractions
you might have survived the nineteenth century,
domesticating your grief into a nostalgia
for seashores or mountains. You might have drifted
into a T-shirted life of rented rooms, eating out of bags
at tables littered with pamphlets and timing devices.
You might have danced on the Wall the night it crumbled
into history. You might have loved again,

married a kindergarten teacher,
joined a brokerage firm exploiting the East, crept from bed
to watch Serbian war pornography smuggled out of Banja Luka
or a documentary on four greasers in Hamburg
singing "Sie Liebt Dich," tormenting you with visions
of Charlotte, that equivocating whore
for whom you almost squandered your future.
Such was her web.

—Upon me also, dark patches fell. Live all you can.
It's a mistake not to. I betrayed my desires to hidden cameras,
too much *Sturm und Drang* for a life of laundry and newspapers,
the life you couldn't bear to live, beyond whose dreams
lies Death, the near abroad.
Werther, the grids of Europe are dimming.
I think of you tonight in this darkness of more than a kitchen,
groping for more than a match.

The Cloisters

I'd forgotten the erotic ambiance of that A train to the Cloisters
after you deconstructed Edward Hopper at the Whitney.
A lascivious angel danced over the heads of the perpetually unchaste

as you described how one young thing (a thick-ankled blonde
standing in a doorway) looked as if she'd been knocked up by a god,
her life captured in all its sun-drenched vacancy.

We were different. Ours was the case history of a man
unable to behave divinely, though I remember the warmth of your body
behind those quince trees in the courtyard.

All these years I've kept your Marxist bibliography
in my wallet, afraid to destroy it until its relevance expired.
I still revere you but it's time to say goodbye Lukacs, goodbye Foucault:

what's worth saving can't be saved, having died as we walked
the stations of the cross under a cold March sun that never burst
into revelatory light, smoldering ineffectually behind persistent clouds.

I'VE CULTIVATED A NOSTALGIA

I've cultivated a nostalgia so frugal it re-lives
the death of Communism without party favors or vodka, your
embryo taking root

and Ceausescu executed within hours
of each other on a Christmas morning
five years down the road from this consensual foot massage

in the balcony of the recital hall,
our pleasure advancing without resistance, our souls
privy to a sense of scale that makes a flea circus out of history.

My Glass of Spinoza

Perjurers recant their testimony in hell
but I'm in a clam bar chasing angels on horseback.
The waiter despises me and I return the favor,
an equipoise through which I find my audience,
for who but the insufferable deny the virtues of antagonism?

It is midnight. The seals are barking.
Drunk on the ethics of wine,
I raise my glass of Spinoza to the judge,
a Holocaust survivor who feigned displeasure
when I described your voice as velvet-on-the-brain.

Though whatever else I said was false at least *that* was true—
not that it mattered to the lone harpooner
on that jury of whale-watchers,
a creature of impulse unacquainted with remorse:
no backward glances, no premonitions beyond the buoys.

If I Must Be Saved

A spacious night, the ward quiet but for a male nurse humming
Klezmer music to your roommate, an elderly Polish
widow suffering in body only, her roofless
mind deluged by grace
as the first priest to orbit Earth
administers extreme unction to New York City,
its helium balloon of Christ punctured beyond repair
and dying in the orange and brown floodlights of Thanksgiving.

If I must be saved, let it be from the world to come.
Though it is wrong to twist silence into forgiveness
I'm tired of waiting for absolution.
If this is really you sleeping next to John's roses,
tell me quick why God fails the just and love dies—tell me quick
before this night slips westward against my will.

BOOKS FROM ETRUSCAN PRESS

Synergos | Roberto Manzano

Lies Will Take You Somewhere | Sheila Schwartz

Legible Heavens | H. L. Hix

A Poetics of Hiroshima | William Heyen

Saint Joe's Passion | J. D. Schraffenberger

American Fugue | Alexis Stamatis

Drift Ice | Jennifer Atkinson

The Widening | Carol Moldaw

Parallel Lives | Michael Lind

God Bless: A Political/Poetic Discourse | H. L. Hix

Chromatic | H. L. Hix (National Book Award finalist)

The Confessions of Doc Williams & Other Poems | William Heyen

Art into Life | Frederick R. Karl

Shadows of Houses | H. L. Hix

The White Horse: A Colombian Journey | Diane Thiel

Wild and Whirling Words: A Poetic Conversation | H. L. Hix

Shoah Train | William Heyen (National Book Award finalist)

Crow Man | Tom Bailey

As Easy As Lying: Essay s on Poetry | H. L. Hix

Cinder | Bruce Bond

Free Concert: New and Selected Poems | Milton Kessler

September 11, 2001: American Writers Respond | William Heyen

etruscan press

www.etruscanpress.org

Etruscan Press books may be ordered from:

Consortium Book Sales and Distribution

800-283-3572

www.cbsd.com

Small Press Distribution

800-869-7553

www.spdbooks.com